Andrew Pegler is a freelance journalist and writer best
known as writer, editor and publisher of *The St Kilda Bugle*,
a satirical newspaper that reports on the ludicrous
happenings in a small imaginary community.
This is his first book and he hopes you enjoy it.

Acknowledgements

This book was an enormous research project made easier
by the following resources:
www.truthoverboard.com
www.sievx.com
www.cpa.org.au
www.melbourne.indymedia.org
www.australianpolitics.com

The office of Michael Danby Federal Member
for Melbourne Ports; Anne Cabrié

Australia Deserves Better Than John Howard published by the ALP in
1997; *The Howard Record* published by the ALP 1996; *Dark Victory* by
David Marr and Marian Wilkinson, Allen & Unwin; *Hansard*

A special thanks also to Alex Tyers for the great illustrations,
Shireen Nolan at De Luxe and Associates who went at it like
a Trojan and James De Vries for taking it on in the first place.
You all rok!!

John Howard's Little
Book of Truth

PUBLISHED IN 2003 BY HARDIE GRANT BOOKS
12 CLAREMONT ST, SOUTH YARRA, VICTORIA 3141,
AUSTRALIA WWW.HARDIEGRANT.COM.AU
NATIONAL LIBRARY OF AUSTRALIA
CATALOGUING-IN-PUBLICATION DATA:
A CATALOGUE RECORD FOR THIS BOOK IS AVAILABLE
FROM THE NATIONAL LIBRARY OF AUSTRALIA.
EDITED BY MARTINE LLEONART
COVER AND TEXT DESIGN BY DE LUXE & ASSOCIATES
PRINTED & BOUND IN AUSTRALIA BY GRIFFIN PRESS
EVERY EFFORT HAS BEEN MADE TO INCORPORATE
CORRECT INFORMATION AND STATISTICS. THE
PUBLISHERS REGRET ANY ERRORS AND OMISSIONS,
AND INVITE READERS TO CONTRIBUTE UP-TO-DATE
OR ADDITIONAL RELEVANT INFORMATION TO HARDIE
GRANT BOOKS.
10 9 8 7 6 5 4 3 2 1

John Howard's Little Book of Truth

ANDREW PEGLER
Illustrated by Alex Tyers

Hardie Grant Books

For the majority of us life's a stolid metronome from womb to tomb, a cloistered meander on a mortal escalator towards an imperceptible vacuum created by our demise. Opportunities pile up behind the couch with loose change and dusty morsels of pizza. God is the comedian and we are an audience too afraid to laugh. But don't worry because experience and wisdom are the spawn of trial and suffering, they build the soul's endurance. As Nietzsche muttered through a syphilitic haze, "What does not kill me only make me stronger."

For the remaining few there's Federal politics and this book is for you guys.

Cheers,
Andrew Pegler

~CONTENTS~

Political language
is designed to
make lies sound
truthful and murder
respectable and
to give an appearance
of solidity to pure wind

George Orwell

MY GOVER
WILL ALW
TO BE TRU
OPEN WIT
AUSTRALI

John Howard, Prime Minister of Australia

NMENT
AYS SEEK
THFUL AND
H THE
AN PUBLIC

~CHAPTER I~

A Certain Maritime Incident

~*Truth Overboard*~

The "Children Overboard Affair", in which the Government accused asylum seekers of throwing their children into the sea in early October 2001, came at the early stages of the federal election campaign. Public mistrust, fear and anger of asylum seekers became unprecedented. The Liberals were voted back in and commentators now refer to this as John Howard playing "the race card".

WHOOPS!

interj, an explanation indicating mild dismay or surprise

"In an election campaign, as at any other time, I owe the
Australian people an obligation to be truthful. I discharged
that obligation because what I said about this issue was to
my knowledge correct. Although I acted in good faith on
the basis of advice, I do regret it if anyone now feels that
they were misled."
John Howard February, 2002

UMMMM ERRRRR

interj, an indication of hesitation or inarticulateness

"I haven't seen it (the video of the incident), I've been told of it by Mr Reith. I've got a lot of things to see at the present time. I don't know that there is a particular need at this stage to make it public."
John Howard 26 October, 2002

"Mr Reith did not tell me of doubts over the children
overboard claims"
John Howard 15 February, 2002

Reith is told in Darwin by Brigadier Silverstone that the
video does not show children in the water. He replies:
"Well we'd better not see the video!"
 9 October, 2002

When the public demanded proof Peter Reith released
a few photos showing images of flayling asylum seekers.
The photos "Laura the hero" and "Dogs and his family"
appear with their explanatory text, including the date the
photos were taken, removed.
10 October, 2002

AH OH...

interj, an exclamation expressing pain, surprise, complaint, dislike.

"By 1100 on 11 October 2001, Mr Reith and a
number of his senior advisers had been informed that
the photographs released the previous day did not depict
children in the water after having been thrown overboard
on 7 October."

Bryant Report, page ix

I dont know how

"There was nothing to suggest that women and children
had been thrown into the water"
*Acting Chief of the Defence Forces Angus Houston to Peter Reith,
in phone conversation witnessed by Brigadier Gary Bornholt on
7 November, 2001.*

Mr Reith does business.

*Brigadier Gary Bornholt, 16 Feburary, 2002.
and most likely asked by anyone aged over six.*

"I have now reached the conclusion that there is no
evidence to support the claim that children were
thrown overboard"
Admiral Barrie 27 February, 2002

On 21 February, 2002 Peter Reith admits to having been told on 7 November that children overboard claims were false. Mr Howard claims not to have been told of this by Reith despite specifically asking him about it on 7 November.

"My experience in relation to Peter Reith, and I say this unqualifiedly, is that I always found Peter Reith to be a man of great decency and honour."
John Howard

MR SPEAKER!

"Mr Jordana did tell me that he believed that he may have
been told by someone in the former Defence Minister's
office and perhaps by Jane Halton... that there were
unsubstantiated rumours in Defence regarding the
juxtaposition of the dates on the photographs."
"... as those were simply unsubstantiated rumours,
he did not raise the matter with me."
John Howard at Question Time 18 February, 2002

"If the Defence Minister and Immigration Minister get verbal advice from Defence sources and the Prime Minister gets that kind of written advice I don't think it's sort of exaggerating or gilding the lily to go out and say what I said"
John Howard 8 November, 2001

CHAPTER 2

Waiter! There's a Tax in my Soup

~The GST~

The Goods and Services Tax was a funny one. One moment it was "dead in the water" the next we're all filling in a BAS statement.

LEST WE FORGET

"There is no way a GST will ever be part of our policy.
Never, ever. It's dead, it was killed by the voters in the
last election."

John Howard media conference, Tweed Heads Civic Centre, May 1995

"My government will not introduce any new taxes, and will not increase existing taxes"

John Howard 1996
(said just before the 1996 election)

"My fellow Australians, may I have a few moments of
your time to say why the new tax system which starts
on Saturday is good for Australia."
John Howard, address to the nation June, 2000

ERR

v.i. to go astray in thought or belief

"There is absolutely nothing wrong with stating a
position on something, honoring that during the
term of government then altering your opinion and
going to the public again with that altered opinion."
John Howard The Australian, *May, 1998*

"I think when people see the GST come in and see the new tax arrangement they will be very satisfied."
John Howard 29 June, 2000

"The GST will not increase the price of petrol for the ordinary motorist"
John Howard address to the Nation, 13 August, 1998

ACTUALLY

adv. as an actual or existing fact; really

When the GST was introduced fuel excise was cut by 6.7
cents a litre but the GST added 8.2 cents per litre, a net
increase of 1.5 cents per litre.

"A coalition government will slash the burden of paper work and regulations on small business with our aim being a 50% reduction in our first term of office."
Liberal Party Press release, 1996

BUT...

The tax act is now nudging

10,000 PAGES.

Tax assessment for wage and salary earners has become very difficult. Plus, small businesses have to do four BAS statements a year.

Simplification of the tax system is what we all want.

The Tax Pack instructions ballooned to 350 pages in size. The individual tax return form has grown in size from six pages in 1996 to 12 after introduction of the GST.

"Pensioners will be better off under a GST. If you are over 60 you will get a $1000 bonus."

Forty per cent of them got nothing. Under the 'Savings Reward Scheme' pensioners were rewarded for savings, with a promise of up to $1000 dollars. But to get it they had to have large savings. Those that had money were fine, those that did not got hammered.

Janette was surprised to find a nude photo of President George Bush in her husband's wallet.

There are no facts,
only interpretations

Friedrich Nietzsche

Waiter! There's a Blair in my soup!

~CHAPTER 3~

Along for the Ride

~The Iraq War~

WE WON'T JUST AUTO -MATICALLY CLICK OUR HEELS AND F✶LL✶W THE AMERICANS

John Howard 27 September, 2002

**Meanwhile back at the ranch:
"Has anyone seen John?"**

Was Iraq or Afghanistan a threat to us? Failure so far to find evidence raises questions about the doctrine of pre-emption (which has a lot to do with the way Dubbya made his decision). Anyway, Aussie Johnny just sort of went along for the ride. Meanwhile UK weapons expert Dr Kelly wrote in the *New York Times* of "many dark actors playing games" and claimed a British report on Iraq's WMD had been "sexed up". He committed suicide on 17 July, 2003. Iraq's new fragile political system continues to struggle. Australia has now been named by Jemaah Islamiah and al-Qaeda as an enemy.

"You just don't make decisions like we do and put our nation's youth at risk based upon something that appears not to have existed."

John Howard

John Howard's Little Book of Truth

OBLIQUE

adj, not honest, deceptive, evasive

"We have not found at this point actual weapons"
US weapons inspector David Kay, 2 October, 2003

"We had clear intelligence assessments that Iraq had a weapons of mass destruction capability."
John Howard 3 October, 2003

Apparen

tly not...

"Australian intelligence agencies made it clear to the
Government all along that Iraq did not have a massive
WMD program." *Andrew Wilkie, Senior Intelligence Officer.*
"I will go so far as to say that the material was going
straight from ONA (Office of National Assessments)
to the Prime Minister's Office and the dishonesty was
occurring somewhere in there."
*Andrew Wilkie to a Federal Parliamentary inquiry into
the intelligence on Iraq's weapons of mass destruction, 31 May, 2003*

"The ONA understood months before it commenced
that war was inevitable and Australia would be involved."
Andrew Wilke 31 May, 2003

On 11 March, 2003 Andrew Wilkie resigned in protest
claiming John Howard fabricated material for his case
against the regime of Saddam Hussein.

Coalition of the willing

John Howard characterised Saddam Hussein as a mass murderer, torturer and persecutor of his people who must be removed so Iraqi citizens could be free of his tyranny. When Iraqis sought refuge in Australia they were locked up or turned away.

"There has never been, in my lifetime, a more serious deceit in the Western democracies, including our own, by our leaders, than the argument that was put for the invasion of Iraq."
Greens leader Senator Bob Brown 3 October, 2003

The difference between false memories and true ones is the same as for jewels – it is always the false ones that look the most real, the most brilliant.

Salvador Dali

CHAPTER 4

The Jolly, Gay Ethanol Adventures of John Howard and Dick Honan

I n Mr Downer's math class Little Johnny Howard and Big Dick Honan had been sitting for what seemed an eternity. It was nearly the summer break and rampant fantasies of summer chum fun filled their heads. Up front the rather queer Mr Downer rattled on. "Maths is about figuring out the answer before the question," he droned, before adding he was very fond of small figures and mad keen on Welsh shafting.

Memories of lashings of ginger beer and cake last summer at Ms Vanstone's Confectionary flooded back. "Oh how slow time moves," mumbled Big Dick to Little Johnny. "Oh yes rather," replied Little Johnny. "But just think about the gay time we'll have over summer holiday."

The boys were great friends because Big Dick was a strong supporter of Little Johnny in his role of Captain of lower

school and had helped him campaign all term. And now Big Dick wanted to ask Little Johnny a favour.

You see, his company the Manildra Group was only making 87% of lower school's ethanol and he wanted more. Also he was having problems with those pesky Brazilians from the upper school who were offering the school cheaper ethanol than Big Dick's.

L ittle Johnny had really appreciated Dick's help during term so he decided to help. "I have a jolly good idea," he said. "Let's use school subsidies and other excises to push out those cheaper Brazilians and help secure Manildra millions." That made Dick a very happy chap and he promised to go on helping Johnny in his campaign for reelection as form captain which made Johnny very happy indeed.

But the boys had to keep it a secret from those pesky chaps in White House who were always trying to get them in trouble, especially that nasty Simon Crean.

The two chums then left the classroom and strutted off towards the upper oval where Johnny called a meeting of all class monitors and announced to the chaps that he was introducing ethanol production subsidies and various fuel excises.

All went swimmingly, until Simon Crean's pesky nose for detective work started to suspect something was afoot.
At recess break the next day in front of all the other boys Simon asked Johnny if he had been contacted by a major producer of ethanol or by any representative of his company or the Industry Association before his decision to impose fuel excise on ethanol?

If so, when? And was he urged
to take action to prevent a
shipment of ethanol from Brazil
at a commercially competitive
price being sold to the school?

Johnny had to think fast "I did not personally have discussions with any of them," he said. And hoped that would be the last of it.

Then again at lunch break Simon asked the same question and again Johnny had to lie, "As I stated before, I had not spoken to Dick Honan on this issue."

Then all the chaps in White House started asking Johnny the same question. He was in a fix, "Mmm I have to work out how to get out of this," Johnny said to his friend the ever faithful Max Moore-Wilton, a cheery-faced, eager-eyed youngster. "So let's hatch a plan."

After school the two boys went to Ms Vanstone's Confectionery shop for lashings of ice cream and ginger beer. "Heavens to mergatroyd those damn ingrate White House boys," said Max between mouthfuls. "A smashing bit of detective work though what?" Johnny replied. "Yes but now we must get out of this one so you will be reelected form captain next year," said Max. "Jolly good idea," agreed Johnny.

So the two chaps put their heads together and came up with a brilliant plan and the next day when Simon asked him the same question this is what Johnny said: "What I was asked about at lunch break yesterday specifically related to a shipment of ethanol from Brazil by a company called Trafigura. When I met Dick I didn't know about the shipment, and had not discussed it. That's what I'd meant to say. Sorry chaps."

Although the members of White House were still mad, the whole affair seemed to slip off the radar after the school paper owned by Mr Rupert Murdoch decided not to write anything more about it.

The end.

Lost for words? Scribble down some here...

_____

_____

_____

_____

_____

_____

_____

_____

_____

_____

_____

_____

_____

_____

_____

_____

_____

Our lives begin
to end the day
we become silent
about things
that matter

Martin Luther King

**Janette was surprised to find a nude photo of
Sir Donald Bradman in her husband's wallet.**

~CHAPTER 5~

Historical Bottlers

~Johnny style~

EDUCATION

History is bunk, as someone once said.
Here's proof.

SMEDUCATION

"I promise to maintain the current level
of real expenditure on Austudy."

WELL UNFORTUNATELY

Austudy was cut by $527 million over his first tem.

"The coalition will maintain the level of Commonwealth
funding to universities in terms of operating grants."
November, 1995

Again, operating grants to universities were cut by
$623 million over the first term.

"A coalition government will promote quality and excellence."

Coalition Higher Education policy February, 1996

HEAL✝H

"Medicare will be retained in its entirety."
February, 1996

SMEAL+H

WELL UMMM EEEERR...

There was the abolition of the dental plan and the increase of the co-payment Pharmaceutical Benefit Scheme.
There was $800 million less for public hospitals.

"This nation is clearly heading in the right direction."
John Howard 1 September, 2001

TION !

"The coalition will maintain expenditure on labour market programs." *John Howard February, 1996*

Labour market programs were slashed by $1800 million over the next four years.

"Environmental issues should never be dealt
with as separate from the profitability and
sustainability of our industries."
John Howard February, 1996

JOBS

Howard's great ideas about boats

PTIs: potential illegal immigrants PUAs: possible unauthorised arrivals UAs: unauthorised arrivals UBAs: unauthorised boat arrivals SUNCs: suspected unauthorised non-citizens

Great idea #1

Great idea #2

~CHAPTER 6~

Leaking like a SIEV

~The appalling tragedy of SIEV X~

On 19 October, 2001, Australia was at the mid-point of the election campaign when a hideously overloaded boat carrying 397 asylum seekers sank suddenly in the waters between Java and Christmas Island.

Most drowned quickly.

A hundred or so clung to jetsam.

Twenty hours later two Indonesian fishing boats plucked the 44 asylum seekers still alive.

Three-hundred and fifty-three had died.

146 children
142 women
65 men

"The boat did not sink in Australia Waters"
John Howard 23 October, 2001
Referring to asylum-seeker boat commonly called SIEV X.

An eight-year-old boy lost 21 members of his family.

DUBIOUS

adj. of questionable character, hesitating in opinion

John Howard insisted he had no clear information as to the boat's whereabouts. Subsequent evidence proves they drowned in waters within Australian responsibility. Several Australian government agencies concealed that it went down some ninety miles south of the Sunda Strait (i.e. well inside the saturation surveillance zone of Operation Relex).

John Howard was re-elected.

The Little John Word Finder Puzzle

H	T	A	M	P	A	Z	P	S	E	J
E	O	I	N	K	H	T	H	M	T	D
A	V	W	B	U	S	H	O	A	H	I
L	E	H	A	G	W	B	N	L	A	C
T	R	A	T	R	M	A	E	L	N	K
H	B	N	T	H	D	L	C	H	O	H
C	O	S	L	E	H	D	A	H	L	E
R	A	O	E	I	R	Y	R	N	R	A
I	R	N	R	H	A	R	D	A	E	D
S	D	H	H	H	H	R	O	U	N	J
I	F	E	E	S	H	H	H	R	E	o
S	B	R	A	D	M	A	N	U	G	G

Find and circle the following words in the fun puzzle above

- HOWARD
- GST
- TAMPA
- LIAR
- OVERBOARD
- PHONECARD
- HEALTHCRISIS
- WMD
- BALDY
- BATTLER
- TERROR
- BUSH
- NAURU
- SOLUTION
- GG
- HANSON
- BRADMAN
- DICKHEAD
- FEES
- ETHANOL
- RENEG
- SMALL
- JOG
- OINK

Lost for words? Scribble down some here...

- Minion Porkies -

~Subordinates Behaving Badly~

Behind every great PM there is a minion
with a porkie. These fellas and gals form
the bedrock on which the political landscape
of this great country rests. This is devoted to
them and stars minions overboard, the *SIEV*
porkies and one about the stolen generation.

Minions Overboard

"Disturbingly a number of children have been thrown overboard, again with the intention of putting us under duress. (It was) clearly planned and premeditated. People wouldn't have come wearing life jackets unless they intended some action of this sort."

Philip Ruddock 7 October, 2001

"Well, it did happen. The fact is the children were thrown into the water. We got that report within hours of that happening."
Peter Reith 10 October, 2001

"That there was a certain determination on the part of the people to make sure they were taken onboard was evidenced by the way they behaved. The extent to which people threw themselves into the water and in some cases it would appear threw their children first – I don't think the children were thrown in later, I think they were thrown in first – it may well have been a parent that followed them in, I don't know. All we know is that children were thrown in and others jumped in."

Philip Ruddock

A Reith doorstep/sidestep interview in Perth around that time

(thanks ABC radio)

Journo: The real issue is why did you take so long to see that video?

Reith: Oh look, I still haven't seen that video.

Journo: But you said [inaudible] that somebody had seen that video and that it definitely showed a child being thrown overboard. Now you are backing away from that now are you?

Reith: No. What I said was that the advice that I had at the time…

Journo: A child had been thrown overboard.

Reith: Excuse me. The advice that I had at the time and the statement that I made was that I had received advice that said that the video confirmed the advice that I had. That's what I said. I had advice from Defence from somebody who had seen the video that they said that it confirmed the advice that I got. Now, that is a true statement at the time then and it's a true statement today. The advice that I had got was that somebody else had seen the video, I had not seen it, still haven't seen it, and that it was confirmation of what I was being told.

OBFUSCATE

v.t., to confuse or stupefy

"The disembarkations were all voluntary."
*Philip Ruddock. Regarding the removal of refugees
from the Manoora, anchored off Nauru, 4 October, 2001*

Immigration Minister Philip Ruddock was told the asylum-seeker vessel *SIEV X* had sunk in international waters – within the zone patrolled by the Australian navy and air force but failed to pass this on to the PM who claimed the *SIEV X* sunk in "Indonesian waters" (so it was outside Australia's responsibility).

"The boat capsized and sank quickly south of the
western end of Java," claimed Jane Halton, Chair of the
Government's People Smuggling Taskforce. Halton later
explained this may have referred to the Indonesian search
and rescue zone. "Our experience of the description of
the Indonesian waters right through this period was,
to say the least, very confused."

On 21 February, 2002 Reith fessed up to having been told children overboard claims were false on 7 November. Basically he was pulling our leg.

He did not deny that he had received information raising doubts about the photos. Reith said he never told Howard even though he spoke to him on the telephone that night.

WHAT?!

"There never was a generation of stolen children."
Minister for Aboriginal and Torres Strait Islander Affairs,
John Herron, in a submission to the Government's response
to the Stolen Generations.

Subordinate SIEV Porkies
How to Deny the Bleeding Obvious 1.01
with Professor Peter Reith.

Reith had just secretly signed a directive to have the *Tampa*
cleared and the ABC had just shown the nation six Iraqis
being dragged off against their will by 30 soldiers.
"Look obviously from their point of view they want to
say this is a shocking business on behalf of Australia; that
they've been forced against their will; that they've been
badly treated. I appreciate that's what some of these people
want to run as an argument. But the advice I have is that it
went reasonable smoothly."

A man was shown being dragged kicking and screaming to a bus. "Well he was a bit difficult." *Peter Reith* The 30 soldiers in full camouflage that surrounded the ship? "We took sensible precautions." *Based on information from David Marr & Marian Wilkinson's* Dark Victory.

RESPONS

IBILITY

adj,
having
a
capacity
for
moral
decisions
and
therefore

= ACCOUNTABLE

CODE
OF
CONDUCT

CHAPTER 8

Ministerial Misconduct

~The Guide on Key Elements of
Ministerial Irresponsibility~

John Howard tabled "The Guide on Key Elements of Ministerial Responsibility" to Parliament in 1996.

NO COMMENT

"The guidelines that are laid down in this document will be complied with in full."

John Howard

SOON AFTER...

Assistant Treasurer Jim Short resigned on 13 October, 1996 after it was found he had approved an operating license for an ANZ Bank subsidiary while holding shares in the ANZ Bank.

WHOOPS!

On 14 October, 1996, the Industry Minister John Moore was forced to defend owning shares in a company called Bligh Ventures and another called Ralston Pty Ltd despite the express prohibition in The Guide on Key Elements of Ministerial Responsibility on Ministers operating as share traders. He survived.

OH!

On 15 October, 1996 Parliamentary Secretary to the Treasurer Brian Gobson resigned after it was found he had exempted a Boral subsidiary from certain provisions of the Corporations Law while holding shares in Boral.

...UMMM ERRR AHHH...

On 11 July, 1997 Small Business Minister Geoff Prosser
was forced to resign when it was found that he owned
three shopping centres and took an active interest in
running them.

and let's not forget...

that same year Minister for Resources and Energy, Warwick
Parer was caught out owning $2 million worth of shares in
resource companies.

That was seven ministers gone in 18 months after
The Guide on Key Elements of Ministerial Responsibility
was tabled.

MMMMM...

And then there was the travel rorts affair...

September 1997, Transport and Regional Development Minister John Sharp resigned for misappropriating travel allowance. Administration Services Minister David Jull resigned on the same day for covering up for him. Science and Technology Minister Peter McGauran resigned a few days later also for misappropriating travel allowance.

All up five ministers, two parliamentary secretaries and
several senior staff members were found to have flouted
The Guide on Key Elements of Ministerial Responsibility.
The cost to John Howard in maintaining such a high
standard was getting too much. To stem the loss of
ministers and secretaries he changed the guide in 1998 to
be just a set of guidelines. Then in 1999 John Howard
introduced a new set of guidelines allowing ministers to
retain ownership of assets relevant to their portfolio as
long as they did not directly manage them.

"This government has adapted clear public guidelines which
  are far more specific than those of former governments."
  John Howard

Ladies and Gentlemen introducing Peter Reith, his Telecard and his toffy son.

In 1994 Peter Reith gave his taxpayer funded Telecard number to his son (and then lost track of it for five years).

On 10 October, 2000, the *Canberra Times* revealed he had a phone bill of $50,000. Reith refused to pay saying he was not responsible for it. It was found Reith had probably known about the bill for about a year and had worked hard to postpone its payment.

Under intense media pressure he revealed he had given the telecard PIN to his son and claimed his son was responsible for $950 worth.

"I simply say this about my son. He's my son, he's a good son. I must say that he thought he could use it from time to time like the phone at home."
Peter Reith 11 October, 2000.

By October 13, 2000 public uproar was so great he was forced to take out a loan and pay all $50,000 back.

A lie gets halfway around the world before the truth has a chance to get its pants on.

Winston Churchill

Sherrif John

HI WILSON

Wilson Tuckey gloated to the ABC Four Corners program that when plotting to destroy the Howard leadership in 1989 he had "lied" to the media. Recently he lied again. According to records he misled the parliament on five occasions claiming his son was a constituent and wrote to the South Australian Police Minister on his Ministerial letterhead in January 2003 to get him off a traffic offence.

BYE WILSON

Following a cabinet reshuffle on 29 September, 2003 Wilson's career has augured into the dirt.

Janette was surprised to find a nude photo of
Sir Peter Hollingsworth in her husband's wallet.

~CHAPTER 9~

Other Non-Core Promises

-Random Ones-

Spin the wheel and see what you can win
in the random revolution of truth.

"My charge as Prime Minister is to make whatever
decisions are in the interest of this country"
John Howard August, 2002

"It's pretty odd to call somebody a liar when they actually laid their policy out before the Australian people."
John Howard, ABC radio, 23 February, 2000

"This campaign of misrepresentation, deliberately designed by the ACTU on the eve of an election, to try and persuade all of the Ansett employees to vote Labor is really dishonest and it's not helping the interests of those people who I am concerned about, I care about them."

At that moment, a short stroll downtown, John Howard's legal representatives stood in court declaring the $10 ticket tax imposed to fund Ansett workers' entitlements (accruing for the government at the rate of $8 million a week) does not belong to the workers. In fact, it is possible 'none will be passed on'.

DIFFERENCE

n. the amount that remains after one quantity is subtracted from another.

"The average Australian is now paying $400 a month
less than what he or she was paying to service the typical
housing loan when we were elected – $400 a month,
and you'll be hearing a bit more of that figure over the
next 18 months."
John Howard 2 August, 2003

In Melbourne, young people saving to buy their first home have seen the bar rise from $801 a month in 1996 to $1822 in 2003.

Interest rates fell a percentage point in that time, yet Commonwealth Bank analysis shows the minimum monthly repayment has risen 127 per cent while household incomes rose only 26 per cent.

"Squeeze on first home buyers", Tim Colebatch, the Age, July 2003

ON AGE

"I will reconsider my position when I turn 64."
John Howard

Howard plays on

ON RACISM

"I don't have a racist bone in my body. It is against everything that I have always sort of believed about the equality of men."
John Howard February, 2000

ON EX-GG

"He (Peter Hollingsworth) is the best man for the job,
there is no reason why he should resign"
John Howard

...pants on fire

ON ERRORS

"One of the errors we have made is that we have operated
on the basis that we cannot afford to be offside (with our
Asian neighbours)." But, said Howard, Australia "has a
particular responsibility to do things above and beyond
in this part of the world".

Howard's Wardrobe

Howard's jogging suit

Howard's Y fronts

Howard's singlet

ON REFERENDUM

"The basis of our rejection of these proposals of the
government puts them forward at a referendum is that
they will reduce the Australian Senate, one of the most
democratically elected chambers in the world."
John Howard 1987

In late 2003 Mr Howard put forward his own proposals to
refashion the senate and curb its power "to make it more
faithfully reflect the will of the people".

"All claims of electoral mandates should be viewed with profound suspicion."
Stanley Bach, author of Platypus and Parliament,
The Australian Senate in Theory and Practice.

INCREASINGLY HONESTY (IN POLITICS) IS BEING SWAMPED BY CYNICAL ELECTION CAMPAIGNS

BASED ON FEAR, OR THE BIG SCARE, OR THE MASSIVE LIE.

John Howard 1995

Howard's End